science
essentials

Books are to be returned on or before
the last date below.

KT-436-631

The perfect **exam revision** guide

inheritance
and evolution

Denise Walker

115523

054194

THE HENLEY COLLEGE LIBRARY

First published in paperback in 2010 by:
Evans Brothers
2a Portman Mansions
Chiltern Street
London W1U 6NR

Series editor:
Harriet Brown

Editor:
Harriet Brown

Design:
Robert Walster
Adam Williams

Illustrations:
Q2A Creative

Printed in China

All rights reserved

© **Evans Brothers Ltd 2006**

British Library Cataloguing in
Publication Data

 Walker, Denise
   Inheritance and evolution. -
(Science essentials. Biology)
    1.Heredity - Juvenile literature
2.Evolution (Biology) -
   Juvenile literature
   I.Title
   576

ISBN: 9780237539757

Contents

Introduction

The variety of life on planet Earth is astounding. Life inhabits almost every corner of the globe, from the hot dry deserts, to the

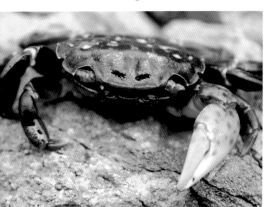

harsh icy poles, and everywhere in-between. For millions of years, species of plants, animals and

microscopic organisms have been adapting their lifestyles to suit their habitats. They have evolved into new species better suited to the environment. Species unable to adapt eventually die out and become extinct. In fact around 99.9 per cent of all organisms that ever existed are now extinct.

In evolutionary terms, humans have only existed on planet Earth for a blink of an eye, but we are very successful. We have evolved from our primitive beginnings into intelligent beings who now dominate the globe.

Each human being is unique. We look and think differently from one another and we pass these characteristics onto the next generation when we reproduce. This is inheritance, and through inheritance we help to create the variation in our species that makes the world such an interesting place to live.

This book guides you through inheritance and explains the fascinating ideas behind natural selection and evolution. It looks at the effect humans can have on evolution and examines how scientists classify and identify species. Feature boxes will help you to unravel more about the mysteries of inheritance and evolution.

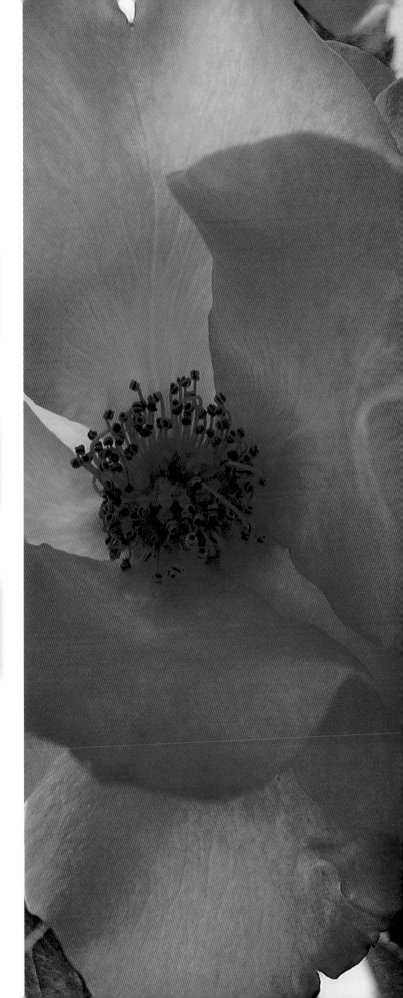

DID YOU KNOW?

▶ Watch out for these boxes – they contain surprising and fascinating facts about inheritance, evolution and classification.

TEST YOURSELF

▶ Use these boxes to see how much you've learnt. Try to answer the questions without looking at the book, but take a look if you are really stuck.

INVESTIGATE

▶ These boxes contain experiments that you can carry out at home. The equipment you will need is usually cheap and easy to find.

TIME TRAVEL

These boxes contain scientific discoveries from the past and fascinating developments that pave the way for the advance of science in the future.

ANSWERS

At the end of this book on pages 46 and 47, you will find the answers to questions from the 'Test yourself' and 'Investigate' boxes.

GLOSSARY

Words highlighted in **bold** are described in detail in the glossary on pages 46 and 47.

What is variation?

In a group of people, such as your class at school or your family, there are similarities and differences between individuals. Each person is a human being with two eyes, two ears and two legs. However, it is our differences, or variations, such as our size, shape and intelligence, which make every one of us unique. Variations are found within any group of animals or plants.

VARIATION

Organisms from the same **species** can reproduce together. Humans are one species and cats are another species. Characteristics such as skin, hair and eye colour, and height and weight, vary a great deal between humans – this is our variation. Variation refers to the differences between individuals or groups of individuals.

Organisms from the same species have less variation than organisms from different species. In other words, two humans have more in common than a human and a cat. There are two main types of variation: **continuous variation** and **discontinuous variation**.

▼ Human beings display a wide variety of variations.

CONTINUOUS VARIATION

Continuous variation occurs when there is a gradual change in a particular feature within a group. For example, look at the people in your class and notice the height differences between you all. A few class members are likely to be very tall, whilst others are very short. However, most of the class fall somewhere between the two extremes. This pattern is repeated with lots of other characteristics, such as foot size and body weight.

If the heights of a group of people of the same age and sex are plotted on a graph, a distinctive curve is produced. This is called a **normal distribution curve**. It shows that a few people are very tall or very short, but the heights of most people fall in the middle. There is a gradual change in height from the shortest to the tallest within the group – this is continuous variation.

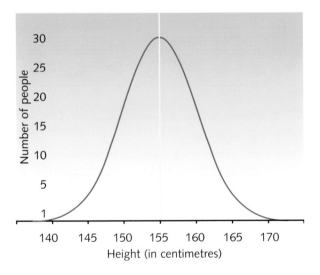

▲ This graph shows a normal distribution curve.

DISCONTINUOUS VARIATION

Discontinuous variation occurs when an individual can be put into one category or another depending on whether or not they have a particular characteristic. For example, the human hairline can have a distinctive peak, called a 'widow's peak'. Individuals either have this characteristic or they do not. We can plot this type of information as a bar chart. Blood group type is another example of discontinuous variation. There are four different blood groups and all human beings belong to one of them.

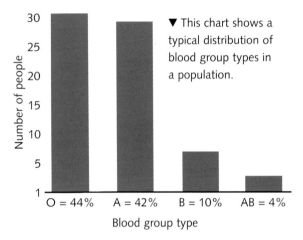

▼ This chart shows a typical distribution of blood group types in a population.

Continuous and discontinuous variations are found throughout nature and can usually be identified by the following rules:
(1) Continuous variation involves features that can be measured, such as height.
(2) Discontinuous variation involves features that can not be measured, such as hairline, blood group and gender.

INVESTIGATE

▶ Do a survey of your class to find out the shoe size of all individuals.
▶ Plot this information on a graph to see if there is a normal distribution curve.

TEST YOURSELF

▶ Write down two more examples of continuous variation.
▶ Write down two more examples of discontinuous variation.

CANINES

Variation does not only occur in human populations. Differences between individuals of the same species exist throughout the animal and plant kingdoms. Consider these two animals (right and below right). What do they have in common? How are they different from one another?

One dog (above right) is a dachshund and has a long back, short legs and short fur. The other dog (below right) is a spaniel, and is easily recognised by its unusually long ears and long fur. Both animals are dogs, but they have quite different characteristics. So what is it that makes these animals dogs?

Animals within a species produce offspring that can also breed together. If spaniels and dachshunds breed, they would produce offspring that would also be capable of breeding. Therefore, spaniels and dachshunds belong to the same species. Animals from different species cannot breed together.

The breeding of dogs with different variations occurs regularly, which is how we end up with mongrels. Mongrels are a combination of different dog types. Any two dogs can

◀ ▲ These two animals are both dogs, but they look very different.

breed with one another as long as one is not huge and the other tiny. Humans have taken advantage of this and have intentionally bred dogs to produce particular variations, such as dogs with long hair, the ability to run fast or a friendly personality.

ROSES

It is not only animals that exhibit variation within a species. Plant species, when naturally cross-bred in the wild, or when deliberately cross-bred by humans, show variation. For example, the variations of a rose species include flower colour, speed of growth and size. Look at the photographs of the two roses. What do they have in common? What are their differences?

The two plants can breed with each other to produce offspring.

◀ This rose has large yellow petals.

The offspring could have characteristics from one of the parent plants or both. Gardeners cross-breed plants to achieve particular variations. For example, if a gardener wants to produce a large rose bush with a yellow flower, he would choose one large bush and one with yellow flowers and breed them; the offspring are called hybrids. It is likely that one of the hybrids would be large and have yellow flowers.

Animals and plants within a species can be naturally or artificially varied. However, they must retain enough characteristics in common to allow the species to reproduce and create future generations. If there are so many changes in a population that individuals from the new and the old populations could not breed together to create future generations, a new species has been created (see pages 24-25).

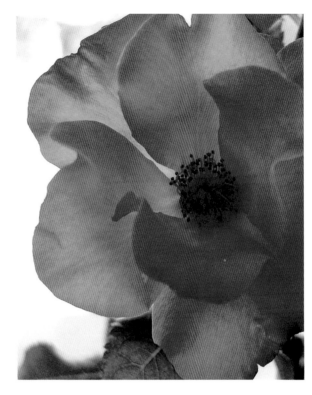

▲ This rose looks different to the flower on the opposite page, yet they are both roses.

DID YOU KNOW?

▶ A horse can breed with a donkey to produce a mule (right). Mules cannot breed.
▶ In the 1960s, Michigan State University biologist Guy Bush studied differences in fruit fly populations. The fruit fly population originally lived, fed and mated on the fruit of hawthorn trees. However, some flies from the population developed a taste for apples and moved to a nearby apple tree. Bush was convinced that the two groups could no longer breed. In the 1980s, researchers identified differences between the two populations, which showed that the groups had not been mating for many generations. They had become different species (see page 25).

Genetic variation and inheritance

Individuals within a species can be highly varied. They are classed as the same species if they are still able to mate with one another to produce offspring who are also able to reproduce. But why do individuals look different from one another? Animals and plants inherit features from their parents, which affect the way that they look.

GENES

The human body is made of millions of **cells**. Inside each cell is a nucleus. The nucleus contains **genes**, which carry the information that describes the entire structure of the human body. The genes are a combination of information from the father and mother. Inheritance refers to the genes gained from the parents when a new individual is created.

▲ These siblings have inherited their features from their mother and father.

HOW ARE GENES INHERITED?

During reproduction, one egg cell from the mother joins together with one sperm cell from the father to make a new human being. These sex cells contain only one copy of each gene. The rest of the cells in the body contain two copies of each gene. Variants of genes are called **alleles**. For example, when eye colour is inherited, the offspring gains one eye colour allele from the mother, and one eye colour allele from the father. Together, the two alleles determine the eye colour in the offspring.

GENES DESCRIBE FEATURES

Snails belonging to the species *Cepaea nemoralis* either have plain shells or banded shells. There are two alleles that describe this feature. One describes a plain shell and the other describes a banded shell. The allele describing a plain shell is dominant over the

◄ This snail has at least one 'plain shell' allele.

DID YOU KNOW?

▶ This dog (right) has one blue eye and one brown eye. Many animals, including humans, can have one brown and one blue eye. The actress Kate Bosworth and the musician David Bowie have this condition, called heterochromia iridium. It happens when simple genetic patterns are not followed and there is no dominance. Instead, a mixture of alleles or a mutation in an allele for eye colour can result in an individual having two different coloured eyes. Interestingly, such individuals often have hearing problems, which suggests that genes also cause the hearing loss.

▶ The vast majority of the world's population have dark eyes, ranging from light brown to nearly black. Dark eye colour genes are dominant over paler eye colour genes.

allele for a banded shell. The banded allele is therefore recessive. If both alleles are present in a snail, the plain shell is the characteristic that is displayed and is called the **phenotype**. The genetic make-up of the snail is called its **genotype**. The combination of alleles in an individual causes its genetic variation.

▶ This snail has two recessive 'banded shell' alleles.

MUTATIONS CAUSE VARIATIONS

When a gene changes its form suddenly, it will not act as it was supposed to and can give rise to unexpected features. The sudden alteration of a gene is called a **mutation**. Mutations happen by chance in nature and can be caused by exposure to radiation and certain chemicals. Cancers are usually caused by genetic mutations that cause cells to reproduce uncontrollably. Mutations are often harmful, as in cancers, but some mutations have no effect at all, or in rare cases, a beneficial effect. For example, natural mutations have produced particularly woolly sheep. Man has taken advantage of this and has bred from these woolly offspring to increase wool production.

Environmental variation

Genes determine which characteristics plants and animals inherit. However, the surroundings and lifestyle of the individual affect how the inherited characteristics develop. This is called environmental variation. Environmental variation can be caused by factors such as climate, water availability, diet, culture and physical accidents.

ENVIRONMENTAL VARIATION IN PLANTS

Imagine you had a crop of vegetables to grow. To test how the environment affects the plants, you split the crop and plant them in two different places. The first crop receives plenty of water, sunlight and a nutrient-rich soil. These plants grow well and produce large, healthy vegetables. The second crop does not receive enough water or sunlight and is grown in poor soil. These plants are deprived of important environmental factors and only produce small vegetables, or none at all. Even though the plants are genetically very similar, environmental variation results in two very different crops.

ENVIRONMENTAL VARIATION IN TWINS

The environment does not only affect plants, it affects animals, including humans. One way to study the effects of the environment is to examine identical twins. Identical twins have exactly the same genetic information. They grow from a single fertilised egg (one egg that has been fertilised by one sperm), which splits into two individuals.

◀ To grow a high quality crop of vegetables, the environmental conditions must be correct.

Most identical twins are brought up in the same environment and are exposed to the same events and experiences. However, when identical twins are separated at birth, differences between them are due to environmental factors. For example, if one twin is reared in a healthy environment with a good diet and plenty of exercise, and the other reared in a less healthy environment with a lack of food and very little exercise, there is likely to be a clear difference in adult body shape.

▲ Identical twins have exactly the same genes.

AGEING – ENVIRONMENT OR GENES?

In 1986, the Minnesota Twin Study of Adult Development began to identify what causes individual differences in ageing. They discovered that as twins became older, their genes caused changes in their personality and activity levels. However, those that chose an active lifestyle and continued to use their brains remained more alert and had stronger feelings of well-being. Scientists believe that our genes determine many of our features, but the environment also plays an important role in defining who we are.

ENVIRONMENTAL VARIATION OVER TIME

Better conditions can lead to environmental variations over a period of time. Over the last 170 years, the average age of menstruation in females has lowered from 16.5 years to 12 years. Scientists believe this is because living conditions and diets are better. Menstruation in females begins when an individual reaches a certain weight. As conditions have improved, that weight is reached sooner and so the age of menstruation has decreased.

Adult height has increased since the Second World War (1939-1945). This is particularly spectacular in Japan. During the years following the war, living conditions for young people improved, which led to a rapid increase in height of the population over a fairly short time.

DID YOU KNOW?

▶ According to a study of 522 pairs of identical and non-identical twins, optimism (a positive outlook) and pessimism (a negative outlook) are influenced by genes. However, the environment influences only optimism, and not pessimism. This means that the environment and genetics contribute to an optimistic outlook, but pessimism is largely controlled by genes.

▶ Not all identical twins are truly identical. In one pair of identical twins, one twin was healthy and a gymnast, but the other had a genetic condition called muscular dystrophy, and died by the age of 16. This can happen when twins differ in the way that they shut off certain **chromosomes**. This only happens with female identical twins.

Mendel and inheritance

Much of what we know about genes and inheritance has been discovered in the last 50 years. But before this time there was much important work, which provided scientists with a foundation on which to build new discoveries. A key figure in the science of inheritance was Gregor Mendel, an Austrian monk and teacher.

MENDEL AND HIS PEAS

Mendel was born in 1822 and lived in a monastery. Here he was responsible for a small garden plot where he was able to carry out some simple experiments on pea plants. Mendel deliberately chose pea plants because:

(1) They fertilised quickly so he didn't have to wait too long for his results.

▼ Gregor Mendel – the first geneticist.

(2) Male and female parts were present on the same plant.

(3) The plants were easy to keep.

(4) Pure lines were available.

(Pure lines are plants that always produce offspring with the same features as the parent plant. For example, if two tall plants are cross-bred, all the offspring plants will be tall.)

MENDEL'S FIRST EXPERIMENTS

Mendel began to cross his pea plants and came up with some very clear observations that paved the way for understanding inheritance patterns. Mendel crossed pure 'round pea plants' with pure 'wrinkled pea plants'. However many times he did this, all the offspring had round peas and none of them had wrinkled peas. From this, Mendel concluded that information could be passed on from parents to offspring. Today, we know that this information is passed on through our genes.

Mendel also noticed that the pea plants were not a mixture of the characteristics of the parent plants. In other words, none of the plants had a mixture of round and wrinkled peas. When two characteristics were involved, one was always stronger than the other. In this case, the gene for round peas is stronger than the gene for wrinkled peas.

MENDEL'S SECOND EXPERIMENTS

Mendel then crossed plants from this new generation with each other. He found that plants in the following generation were also present in very definite proportions – 75 per cent had round peas and 25 per cent had wrinkled peas. This surprised Mendel since he was able to produce a wrinkled pea plant by crossing two round pea plants.

Mendel concluded that offspring carry information from their parents that does not play any part in their own features. This means that some characteristics are able to 'miss a generation'. In this example, the round pea plants were carrying information about wrinkled peas. Therefore, a wrinkled pea plant can be found in the following generation.

Mendel was one of the first geneticists and his work is still important today. Mendel went further to investigate other features and plants. However, he was not particularly successful as many features have very complicated inheritance patterns.

▲ These round peas are similar to those Mendel used for his revolutionary experiments.

THE RESULTS OF A CROSS BETWEEN A ROUND-PEA PLANT AND A WRINKLED-PEA PLANT

Parents	Pure round peas	Pure wrinkled peas
First generation	Round peas Round peas	Round peas Round peas
Second generation	Round peas Round peas	Round peas Wrinkled peas

THE HENLEY COLLEGE LIBRARY

Genetics explored

Our genes describe the features that we inherit. Genes are passed on to us from both our mother and our father. We do not often show an average of our parents' characteristics, but instead can adopt one feature or another. Using the ideas presented by Gregor Mendel's experiments, we can investigate how characteristics are passed on and predict the likelihood of inheriting certain features.

FREE EARLOBES OR ATTACHED EARLOBES?

Take a look in the mirror at your earlobes – do they hang down away from your head, or are they attached? Imagine two people decide to have children. One parent has free earlobes and the other parent has attached earlobes. What type will the child have? Firstly, it is important to understand that we can't predict exactly what will happen; we can only predict the probability of gaining one feature or another.

◀ Free earlobes
▼ Attached earlobes

Sex cells contain half the genetic information of all the other cells (see pages 10-11). In our example, we can represent the allele for free earlobes with 'E' and attached earlobes with 'e'. The parent with free earlobes has two E alleles and the sex cells will each contain one E allele (top row of the inheritance square, below). The parent with attached earlobes has two e alleles and the sex cells of this parent each contain one e allele (the left hand column of the inheritance square, below).

When the sex cells join, one E allele comes together with one e allele, and the individual will have the earlobes dictated by Ee. We know that free earlobes (E) are dominant to attached earlobes (e), so all children from this couple will have free earlobes. This can be summarised in an inheritance square (below) and indicates that all offspring of this couple will have free earlobes.

	E	E
e	Ee Free earlobes	Ee Free earlobes
e	Ee Free earlobes	Ee Free earlobes

▲ This inheritance square shows that all of the offspring of this couple will have earlobes dictated by Ee.

Remember, Gregor Mendel observed the same pattern in his first generation of pea plants (see pages 14-15). Now let us imagine that the parent with free earlobes is a carrier for attached earlobes. This parent has the alleles Ee. The inheritance square now becomes:

	E	e
e	Ee Free earlobes	ee Attached earlobes
e	Ee Free earlobes	ee Attached earlobes

▲ If an E allele and an e allele combine, the offspring will have free earlobes (Ee). If an e allele and another e allele combine, the offspring will have attached earlobes (ee).

In this example, there is a 50 per cent chance that the offspring will have free earlobes and a 50 per cent chance that the offspring will have attached earlobes.

Not all features are dominant or recessive. There are some characteristics that show co-dominance where we end up with an average of the two features. For example, the offspring of parents with different skin pigmentation (colour) can have children with an average of the two skin pigmentations. Hair colour in cattle and horses is inherited in the same way — if red haired and white haired cattle are crossed, the result is called a roan.

▲ This roan horse has white hairs and brown hairs on its neck.

DID YOU KNOW?

▶ Albino people have two recessive alleles for skin pigmentation. Their skin, hair and eyes have little or no melanin. Melanin is a pigment (coloured chemical). Albino people always have vision problems.

INVESTIGATE

▶ Gregor Mendel also crossed tall and dwarf pea plants. The 'tall' allele (T) is dominant to the 'dwarf' (t) allele. For each of the following pairs of plants, draw an inheritance square and work out the probability of gaining tall and dwarf plants.

- Tt and Tt
- TT and tt
- TT and Tt

Time travel: The mysterious shape of DNA

Genes are made of a molecule called DNA (deoxyribonucleic acid). DNA carries all the genetic information that we have inherited from our parents. It is found inside the nucleus of our cells and if we reproduce, we pass on our DNA to our offspring. By determining the structure of the DNA molecule, scientists hoped to gain a deeper understanding of inheritance. As it turned out, uncovering the shape of the DNA molecule was not an easy task.

X-ray photography

Maurice Wilkins, James Watson, Francis Crick and Rosalind Franklin were the four key players in the discovery of the shape of DNA. In the early 1950s, Maurice Wilkins and Rosalind Franklin were working on a technique called x-ray diffraction at King's College in London, UK. This technique involves firing x-rays at samples of DNA. When the x-rays hit the sample, they are sent in different directions producing a scattering pattern. The pattern is recorded onto photographic paper.

Piecing the puzzle together

Meanwhile, James Watson and Francis Crick were working together in Cambridge, in the UK. James Watson was an American geneticist and Francis Crick was a British physicist. Watson and Crick used

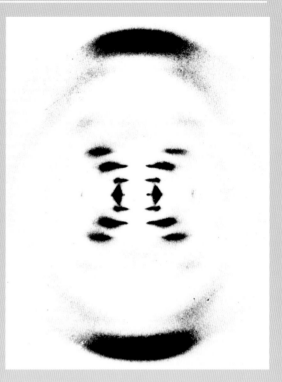

▲ This is the pattern formed on photographic paper by x-rays that have bounced off DNA.

Wilkins' and Franklin's x-ray data to help them build models of possible DNA structures. The x-ray photographs had given them clues to the shape of DNA, such as the distance between certain points in the DNA structure and the length of various portions of the molecule.

Because the shape of DNA was not like any other known biological structure, the interpretation of the evidence was extremely difficult. Watson and Crick often found that each time they changed the structure, not all the clues fitted properly. This was a frustrating and trying time for them.

DNA – A DOUBLE HELIX

Eventually Watson and Crick came upon the correct shape – called a double helix. They knew that they had discovered the correct structure when all the clues fitted like a glove. A double helix is like a spiral staircase. What is clever about this shape is that the DNA can unzip itself along the middle of the 'steps' and each 'banister' of the DNA can copy itself. This is how we end up with copies of DNA in all of our cells.

Our genetic information is actually carried on the 'steps' of the DNA molecule. There are four different chemicals that form the steps – adenine, thymine, cytosine and guanine. Two chemicals pair up to form one step. The way in which they pair up forms a genetic code (genes), which carries instructions for all of our characteristics.

THE NOBEL PRIZE

In 1962, Francis Crick, James Watson and Maurice Wilkins were awarded the highly respected Nobel Prize for their work on uncovering the structure of DNA. Sadly, Rosalind Franklin died in 1958 and did not live to receive an award. The discovery of the structure of DNA has given us a far greater understanding of genetics. Watson went on to head the Human Genome Project (see pages 20-21), which aimed to uncover all the genes found in humans. This project was completed and published in 2003.

▲ This is a computer-generated drawing of the structure of DNA. The shape is called a double helix. DNA is invisible to the naked eye.

Time travel: The Human Genome Project

In 1990, an international team of scientists from the UK, the USA, France, Germany, China and Japan set out to uncover the human genome. The human genome is the total of all the genetic information (genes) held in the cells of the human body. DNA molecules carry this information (see pages 18-19). The team aimed to explain what each part of the DNA molecule was responsible for. The results of the Human Genome Project were published in 2003, but the huge task of analysing all the information is still ongoing.

▲ This is the logo for the Human Genome Project.

RIVALRY

Before the 1990s, other teams of scientists had unravelled the genome for much simpler organisms, such as bacteria and yeast, but mapping the human genome was a far greater task. A private group claimed they would reveal the human genome within months, threatening the international project. They also claimed that when they had done this, they would charge anyone who wanted access to the information. Finally, both the private and international teams published the human genome in 2003. Fortunately, although both teams have continued to work in this field, the information is free of charge to its users.

▼ An IBM supercomputer, similar to this one, is used to analyse the human genome information.

WHY IS THE HUMAN GENOME SO IMPORTANT?

Since the structure of DNA was discovered (see pages 18-19), scientists have believed that certain traits and diseases are inherited through our genes. A full understanding of the human genome means that scientists are closer to knowing which gene, or genes, are responsible for which traits and diseases. Therefore, if a disease is inherited, scientists may be able to pinpoint the gene responsible. For example, women with a certain type of breast cancer carry a particular mutated gene.

GENE THERAPY

Scientists have developed a technique called 'gene therapy' to attempt to cure damaged and mutated genes to prevent development of certain diseases. To date, this technique has been used with some success, and it is a fast-moving area of research. The ultimate aim is to use the human genome to discover new ways of treating, diagnosing and perhaps one day preventing thousands of human disorders.

GENETIC TESTING

The genetic testing of embryos is one of many controversial issues connected with the Human Genome Project. In a genetic test, scientists scan a DNA sample for mutations that indicate that the embryo may develop a disease.

Imagine a situation where a couple want a child and are able to have their embryos genetically tested before being implanted into the female for a pregnancy. If the genetic test shows that the embryo is not perfect in some way, should the couple be allowed to reject it? How far should people be allowed to 'design' their own children? There are those that agree with embryonic genetic testing. They believe that if there is a way of curing otherwise incurable diseases then why should we not do so?

Others believe that it is wrong to tamper with nature in this way and that we need limits on such testing. For example, some believe that it is acceptable to prevent illness, but that it is wrong to choose the eye

▲ How do you feel about genetic testing on human embryos?

or hair colour of a child. This area of genetics is one that will be debated for many years to come. However, a further problem is that the debate about genetic testing does not move as fast as the research itself.

A NEW VIEW OF LIFE

Scientists now have a 'parts list' for how an organism operates, maintains and reproduces itself. What is largely unknown is the function of most genes and how cells in the body use the information from the DNA to come alive. It is likely that future research will not look at individual genes, but rather it will look at systems as a whole. Research on this much grander scale will look at how genes behave in particular environments, how groups of genes act in tissues and organs, and how thousands of genes interact to create 'life'.

Natural selection

You may have heard the phrase 'survival of the fittest'. This means that only the healthiest organisms, or those best suited to their environment, live long enough to pass their characteristics on to the next generation. For example, some organisms have skin or fur that blends in well with their surroundings so predators cannot easily see them. Others only come out at night when there is less danger of being preyed upon. Clearly these organisms have characteristics or lifestyles that help them beat their competitors in the survival game. If they live long enough to reproduce, they will pass on these characteristics to their descendants. We call this trend **natural selection**.

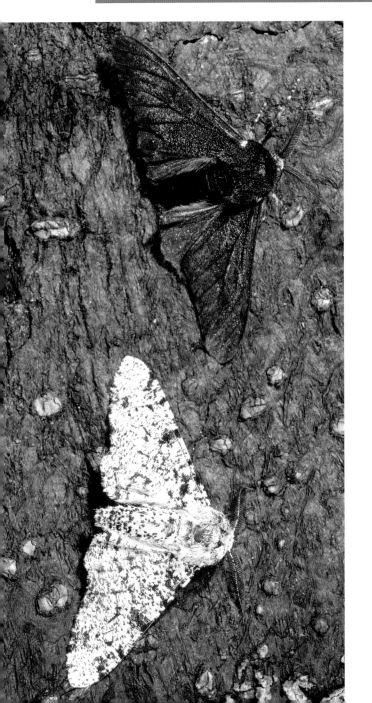

NATURAL SELECTION OF THE PEPPERED MOTH

A famous example of natural selection occurred in the UK in the 1800s. There are two varieties of peppered moth; one is dark grey and the other is paler and speckled. Both varieties of peppered moth feed at night and are preyed upon by birds during the day. To avoid being eaten in the daytime, the moths rest on tree trunks, which provide them with camouflage.

In the early 1800s, the speckled moth population was large, but dark moths were rare. The dark form could be easily seen on tree trunks and made excellent prey for birds. However, during the 1800s many forests were cut down and factories were built in their place. The factories churned out large quantities of soot, which discoloured buildings and plant life. The discoloured buildings and trees provided new camouflage for the dark moth as it could 'hide' itself during the day.

By the end of the 1800s, the dark moth population had grown massively, and speckled moths had become quite rare. The dark moths were living long enough to reproduce and pass on their genes to their offspring. At the same time, the speckled moths suffered greater predation and often did not survive long enough to reproduce.

◀ The dark moth is well camouflaged on this sooty tree trunk. The pale moth is easily seen and eaten by predators.

NATURAL SELECTION IN PEACOCKS

Male peacocks have huge, brightly coloured tail feathers, which are used to impress and attract a mate. The tail feathers also make it difficult for the peacock to escape predators. If the male is able to live long enough to mate and produce offspring, he is likely to be a very strong specimen. In this way, the genes that indicate his 'fitness' for survival and his brightly coloured tail feathers are passed on. This type of natural selection is called sexual selection.

▶ This peacock is indicating he is a strong individual.

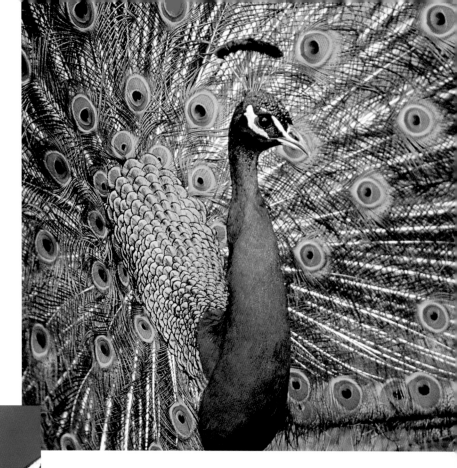

NATURAL SELECTION IN PLANTS

Many plant species have coloured petals and sweet scents to attract insects. These features are present as a result of natural selection. The plants that attract the most insects spread their pollen (sex cells) to a large number of other plants. The offspring of such plants will also carry the genes that describe bright petals and a sweet scent. Therefore, the trait is selected and conserved in future generations. There are also countless numbers of species that have been unsuccessful in their adaptation. Such organisms are now **extinct** (see pages 38-41).

◀ This flower ensures the survival of its species by attracting insects.

INVESTIGATE

▶ Find out which features or abilities the following animals have developed as a result of natural selection to ensure the long-term survival of their species: (1) lions and (2) chameleons

CHARLES DARWIN

Charles Darwin (1809-1882) was a British naturalist who became famous for proposing the theory of **evolution** by natural selection (see pages 22-23). Darwin studied animal and plant life across the globe, particularly in the Galapagos Islands. He came to the conclusion that all life on Earth evolved (developed gradually) over millions of years from a few common ancestors by the process of natural selection. But what led him to believe this?

DARWIN'S FIVE-YEAR VOYAGE

In 1831, Darwin sailed off on HMS Beagle on a round-the-world voyage. During his five-year journey, Darwin spent time studying wildlife on the Galapagos Islands, which are located 960 kilometres off the coast of Ecuador, South America. He observed, collected, recorded and described hundreds of fossils, rocks, fish, insects, plants, birds and mammals throughout the journey. He also sent many samples back home to England.

IMPORTANT DISCOVERIES

Upon Darwin's return in 1836, an ornithologist (bird scientist) called John Gould at the London Zoo Museum took up the study of various bird samples that Darwin had sent him. Darwin thought that the birds were entirely different species – wrens, blackbirds and finches – but John Gould discovered that they were all distinct species of finch.

Darwin studied the finches further and realised that they had obvious differences depending on the island from which they came. The finches from some of the Galapagos Islands had curved beaks, which were ideal for feeding on vegetarian matter. Finches from other Galapagos Islands had straight beaks, ideal for pecking at insects on tree bark.

▼ The Galapagos Islands are home to many weird and wonderful creatures, such as these iguanas.

DARWIN'S THEORY

For the next 20 years, Darwin thought long and hard about the finches and all the other creatures that he had studied and observed. He eventually came to the conclusion that all species were on the Earth through a gradual change over millions of years by the process of natural selection. For this to take place, you need three things:

(1) The organisms must be able to reproduce.
(2) There must be a source of variation (see pages 6-13). For example, a genetic mutation is the likely original cause of the change in beak shape in Darwin's finches.
(3) 'Survival of the fittest' must occur, which means that the best individuals reproduce. The finches with the best beak shape for getting food on their particular island were the 'fittest' and lived long enough to reproduce.

Eventually the different populations of finches changed so much that they became new species. This is known as **speciation**.

DARWIN'S BOOK

Alfred Wallace, a young British naturalist, collected animals in Malaysia where he lived and had drawn the same conclusions as Darwin. Once Darwin realised this, he worked long hours to write his book and publish his ideas on natural selection and evolution. Finally, in 1859, some 23 years after returning from his voyage, he published his famous book 'The Origin of Species by Means of Natural Selection'.

◄ These finch species developed different beak shapes depending on the available food sources.

OUTRAGE

Darwin published his ideas in Britain at a time when the church was very powerful and influential. What Darwin proposed caused an outrage because it conflicted with the belief that God created all creatures. Darwin risked becoming a social outcast. Today, the conflict between evolutionary ideas and religion often centres on 'creationism' or 'intelligent design'. People who believe the Bible is literally true find Darwin's ideas do not agree with their religious views, and maintain instead that all species were created in one go. However, 150 years since the publication of his life's work, Darwin's theories are overwhelmingly accepted by the scientific community.

▼ The beak of this woodpecker finch is perfectly suited to hold a stick, which it uses to extract insects from the tree bark.

Artificial selection

The process of natural selection results in the survival of those organisms with the 'best' features. This allows them to reproduce and pass their desirable genes to their offspring. However, humans often control the breeding of animals and plants to obtain particular variations in the offspring. This is called **artificial selection**.

ARTIFICIAL SELECTION IN PLANTS

Gardeners and farmers often look for plants or crops that will produce either a good yield, or have flowers for a long period of time. This is not easy, particularly in winter when daylight hours are reduced and temperatures are low. Plants that grow every year go into a type of hibernation during winter. Gardeners can prolong the yearly 'lifetime' of their plants by putting them into a glasshouse where conditions can be controlled. However, this is not always practical when there are many plants, or when the plants cannot be easily moved. So, growers use artificial selection to create plants that will produce excellent yields or flower for a long time period.

HOW IS THIS DONE?

The winter-flowering pansy can be grown throughout the winter. It is frost resistant and produces flowers in the coldest months of the year. To create such plants, growers choose long-flowering specimens from a normal population and breed them together. Offspring from this cross are observed and those that flower the longest during the winter are selected. Seeds are collected from those plants, germinated and another generation is grown. The process is repeated until the desirable feature has become strong enough in the plant.

This kind of artificial selection procedure can be used to select for a wide variety of different characteristics, depending on the requirements of the gardener or farmer. For example, artificial selection has been used to generate frost-resistant wheat called Marquis wheat. This crop can be grown at colder times of the year than other varieties, which increases its yield.

◄ Winter-flowering pansies produce flowers in the coldest months of the year between October and May.

PROBLEMS WITH ARTIFICIAL SELECTION IN PLANTS

Artificial selection sounds like a harmless process and provides us with plants that are useful for our everyday lives. However, there is one major drawback. As each generation is produced, only a small number of plants are crossed to give the next generation. In this way, the desirable feature is selected but many plants with other good genes are discarded. The plants in each generation become more and more alike and there is a narrowing of what we call the '**gene pool**'.

This can be a big problem when an environmental factor, such as disease or insect-infestation, comes along. Because all of the plants are genetically very similar, if one plant dies, then there is a very high possibility that all of the plants will die. If the gene pool is wider, there are likely to be some plants capable of surviving.

ARTIFICIAL SELECTION IN ANIMALS

Artificial selection is used in the animal world too, and this plays an important role in

producing cattle and sheep for their most desirable characteristics. Breeders aim to produce cattle for their milk or meat, and sheep for their fleece (above).

HOW DOES IT WORK?

The cattle that produce the best milk or meat are bred with each other. This cross can either be carried out naturally, by putting a bull into a field of female cows, or by artificial insemination. This involves the farmers using the sperm (sex cells) of a prize bull to fertilise his cows.

▲ Prize bulls are chosen for desirable characteristics such as their size or strength.

The offspring in this generation are selected for good milk or meat production and are crossed again. The process is much the same as it is in plants, except animals usually take longer to reach maturity and the results of selective crosses take longer to be seen.

Artificial selection creates the same problems in animals as it does in plants. The gene pool narrows and the selected animals may be at risk of disease or disability. Pedigree dogs often suffer from in-bred traits. The bulldog is bred for its wrinkled appearance and wins prizes for this look. However, the wrinkles lead to breathing problems. In addition, intensively reared animals often suffer from disease and illness spreading rapidly through the population as a result of poor conditions and treatment.

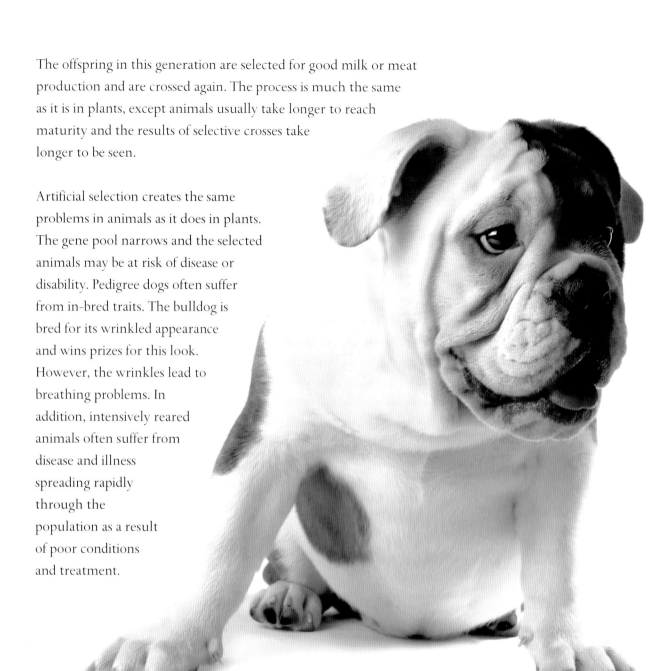

▲ Dogs with wrinkled faces often have breathing problems.

DID YOU KNOW?

▶ In his book 'In the Language of Genes', Steve Jones wrote, "there is little doubt that the most important event in recent human evolution was the invention of the bicycle". But what difference does owning a bicycle make? Before transport systems were invented, no-one travelled very far and marriages were usually between people who lived within a few miles of one another. With the invention of transport systems, couples formed between people who lived in different towns, cities and countries. As a result, genetic mixing happens far more today than it did in the past.

ARTIFICIALLY SELECTED FOX

A farm in Siberia, Russia, has bred a domesticated fox, which looks and behaves just like a pet dog. This selective breeding occurred over a period of just 45 years. Scientists say that the foxes have the ability to follow visual expressions and movements of the hand in much the same way as a domestic dog. They call this behaviour 'social intelligence'.

HOW HAS THE DOMESTIC FOX BEEN BRED?

The domestic foxes are the result of crosses between 100 vixens (females) and 30 male foxes. The foxes, originally from a fur farm, were crossed to select for 'tameness'.
Tests for tameness included:
(1) Seeing whether the foxes would choose to make contact with a human's hand at feeding time.
(2) Seeing whether or not they would bite or run from a human.

After several generations, the scientists noticed that some of the new foxes were distinctly different from the wild foxes. The new foxes were

▲ These baby domestic foxes look a lot like dogs.

eager to receive attention from the human handlers and even whimpered, barked and wagged their tails to attract attention. There were also physical changes. Their coats developed white patches like those of dogs, their snouts became shorter and their ears became more floppy. What is most interesting about this domestication is that it shows us that while we are selecting for one feature, we can at the same time unintentionally select for another feature thought to be completely unrelated. Scientists also hope that the study of these foxes may give clues to the development of social intelligence in humans and other animals.

TEST YOURSELF

▶ Think of some other examples of selective breeding in the plant or animal kingdoms. What is being selected for and why?
▶ For one of these examples, explain how the actual selection could be done.

TIME TRAVEL: STEM CELLS AND CLONING

Scientists have developed an advanced method of artificial selective breeding called **cloning**. This produces individuals that are genetically identical to the 'parent' individual. It is currently illegal to create human clones in most countries, but it is possible to create cloned embryos from which **stem cells** can be taken.

HOW DOES CLONING WORK?

(1) An egg is taken from a donor woman and the nucleus is removed.

Donor egg has its nucleus removed.

The donor egg without its nucleus

(2) An ordinary cell is taken from a second donor, who can be either male or female. The nucleus is removed.

(3) The nucleus from the donor cell in step 2 is placed into the egg cell from step 1. This nucleus contains all the genetic material needed to create the new individual (the discarded egg nucleus only contains half of the necessary genetic material).

The donor nucleus is placed into the empty egg cell.

(4) The egg cell with the donated nucleus is given a short electrical impulse, which causes it to begin dividing to form an embryo.

(5) In theory, the embryo can be implanted into a surrogate mother and allowed to come to full term to produce a cloned human being. This procedure is not permitted in most countries. Research scientists are only allowed to let the embryo divide and grow for up to two weeks. During this time, valuable stem cells are produced.

The egg begins to divide and grow.

WHAT ARE STEM CELLS?

Stem cells are unspecialised cells. They have the remarkable ability to develop into any cell type. Stem cells are present in early human embryos and are very valuable to research scientists. When a stem cell divides, each new cell can either remain as a stem cell, or become a more specialised type of cell, such as a skin or muscle cell.

ADVANTAGES AND DISADVANTAGES

There are many diseases that can affect an individual's quality of life. Parkinson's disease occurs as a result of damage to the nervous tissue. In theory, a patient could donate a nucleus to create a cloned embryo. The stem cells from the cloned embryo could be removed and placed back into the original donor where they could be made to grow into new nervous tissue. Scientists believe

▲ These are stem cells. They are each around 0.01 millimetres in diameter.

that, although a long way off, stem cells could be used to treat a great many diseases. The clear disadvantage of stem cell research is that a new life is created and then destroyed. Many people believe that the destruction of human life at any level of development is wrong.

AN ALTERNATIVE?

Stem cells have also been found in some parts of the human body, such as bone marrow, brain and liver tissue. There are very few stem cells in each type of tissue, but scientists are looking into ways of growing them in the lab. Whether adult stem cells will be a useful medical tool remains to be seen, but early studies are promising.

Heart failure is measured using a quantity called 'ejection fraction'. The ejection fraction is the amount of blood released by the heart with each beat. In healthy people, this quantity is 55 per cent, but in those with severe heart failure, it is less than 35 per cent. In a recent study, adult stem cells were taken from the patients' own hip bones and injected into the damaged heart tissue. After six months, patients who had received stem cells had increased the ejection fraction to 46 per cent. The stem cells appeared to have specialised and become heart muscle cells. Although in its early stages of investigation, it seems that adult stem cells could be used to repair damaged tissues.

▼ This is synthetic bone. Stem cells are put inside it, where they grow into new bone tissue. The new bone is used to repair damaged bones in the human body.

THE HENLEY COLLEGE LIBRARY

8

Evolution uncovered

Charles Darwin's theory states that individuals of a species who are best adapted to their environment will survive long enough to breed and pass on their favourable genes to the next generation. This means that only the fittest will survive and species will gradually change. Some change so much that they form new species. This is the process of evolution by natural selection. Evolution is a gradual process that can take millions of years. It is supported by a huge amount of powerful evidence.

▲ These fossilised fish lived millions of years ago.

FOSSIL EVIDENCE

Fossils are the preserved remains of plants or animals found in rocks. When animals and plants die, they become buried under the ground. Layers of soil and rock build up on top of them and as this happens, the pressure rises. The lower layers are compressed into rocks, which can perfectly preserve the plant and animal remains into fossils. Rocks can be aged using fairly simple techniques and this tells us when the plants and animals found within them lived. Dinosaur skeletons, footprints and even an Ichthyosaur (dinosaur species) embryo inside its mother have been discovered.

One of the most stunning examples of fossilised evolutionary evidence is that of the horse. Fossils tell us that the modern horse evolved from an earlier species called Eohippus, which lived around 60 million years ago. By studying fossilised bones and teeth, we have learnt that the four-toed Eohippus ate leaves from low-hanging branches in forests. Over millions of years, Eohippus evolved into Mesohippus, who had three toes and ate leaves and grass. Pliohippus was the next horse to evolve and had a single-toed hoof and ate mostly grass. Eventually, modern horse, or Equus, evolved. Equus eats grass and has a single-toed hoof. It has longer legs and can run faster than its ancestors.

▲ Mesohippus fossils have been found in the Mid-West of the USA, and in Canada. They lived around 35 million years ago.

GEOGRAPHICAL EVIDENCE

Similar animals and plants are found in similar environments wherever they are in the world. Darwin visited the island of Tristan de Cunha, which lies between Africa and South America. On this island he found plants with features from species found in Africa and South America. Darwin concluded that the island plants were the result of seeds that had been carried by the wind or water from the mainland to the island. Once there, they evolved by natural selection to occupy the specific habitat of the island.

Similarly, rhinoceroses are found on two separate continents – Africa and Asia. It is unlikely that they each formed spontaneously. Instead, fossil records found in different parts of the world show us that today's rhinos are descended from a single common ancestor that lived over 30 million years ago. When the evolution of the ancestor diverged (separated) one line led to the one-horned rhino of India, and the other led to the two-horned rhino of Africa.

▲ The one-horned Asian rhinoceros

▲ The two-horned African rhinoceros

COMPARATIVE ANATOMY

Scientists study and compare parts of animals, such as the heart or feet, to see whether there are any similarities that would indicate a common ancestor. The structures of the hearts of amphibians, reptiles and mammals demonstrate a clear pattern of evolution. The three-chambered amphibian heart has a chamber (1) where all of the blood flowing to and from the heart can mix.

The reptile heart has an incomplete partition, which allows a little mixing. The mammalian heart has a wall that completely separates the heart. This is strong evidence that some amphibians evolved into reptiles, and that some reptiles evolved into mammals. Clearly, a large number of amphibians and reptiles did not evolve further, or they wouldn't exist today.

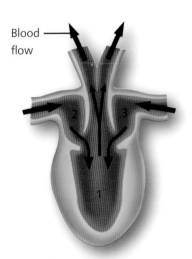

Blood flow

▲ An amphibian's three chambered heart.

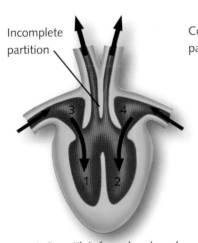

Incomplete partition

▲ A reptile's four chambered heart with incompletely separated chambers.

Complete partition

▲ A mammal's four chambered heart with completely separated chambers.

EMBRYOLOGY

Embryology is the study of organisms and their development from a fertilised egg until they are ready for birth or hatching. It can provide important evolutionary clues. Similarities between species are often seen in embryos but not in the adult form. Embryos of different species that look similar indicate that they may have had a common ancestor. The embryos of a chicken, a pig and a human look strikingly similar. Amongst other features, they all have a head with gill pouches, small limb buds and a tail-like structure.

▼ A pig embryo

▼ A human embryo

▲ A chicken embryo

MOLECULAR EVIDENCE

Almost every organism on Earth contains DNA. DNA is not only the genetic code of an organism; it is also a record of its evolutionary history. By examining DNA molecules, scientists can discover how closely organisms are related. The number of differences in the DNA between two species is directly linked to the length of time since they shared a common ancestor.

Pseudogenes (false genes) are genes that no longer describe a specific function or trait. These are carried in the DNA anyway and are a very useful tool for finding out how closely two

species are related. Some genes exist in two animals because the animals have similar habitats and lifestyles, such as zebras and horses. However, if the same pseudogenes are found in zebras and horses, the only logical explanation is that they have a common ancestor.

The molecular evidence for evolution is overwhelming and in some cases gives us a better description of evolution than other sources of evidence. For example, scientists have long believed that whales are descended from land mammals. They thought that whales were

DID YOU KNOW?

▶ Some scientists believe that three different human species – *Homo sapiens* (modern humans), *Homo neanderthalensis* and *Homo erectus* – co-existed on Earth for about 100,000 years. Traditionally, archaeologists thought that only one human species could exist at a time. In recent years, this belief has been shattered. Fossils prove that several human species occupied Earth at the same time hundreds of thousands of years ago. Today, only modern humans are thought to exist.

related to hoofed creatures, such as cattle, sheep, goats and camels. By studying whales on a molecular level, scientists discovered that their genes that code for milk proteins are very similar to those of a hippopotamus, a hoofed animal. In this case, molecular evidence has enhanced the fossil record and has told us that whales and hippos have a common ancestor.

▼ Hippos and blue whales share a common ancestor.

RECENT EVOLUTION

Bacteria exist in all corners of the Earth. Some of them are harmless and others cause disease. Since the introduction of antibiotics in the mid 1900s, bacteria have evolved strains that are antibiotic resistant. Bacteria change rapidly as a result of mutations and natural selection, and in just one generation can change from being killed by antibiotics to being resistant. This has led scientists to develop many new antibiotics in the hope of staying one step ahead of the bacteria. Equally, the influenza virus evolves each year through mutations and natural selection, meaning that scientists constantly have to create new vaccinations.

TIME TRAVEL: THE HOBBIT OF INDONESIA

Our knowledge of evolution changes all the time, as more and more evidence is uncovered. In September 2004, a group of Australian and Indonesian researchers discovered the bones of a tiny human-like creature buried in a limestone cave on the Indonesian island of Flores. It has been nicknamed the 'hobbit' as it was only one metre tall. This astonishing and controversial discovery has rocked scientists and their understanding of human evolution.

WHAT IS IT?

It was originally believed that the bones belonged to a child. However, investigation of the teeth shows that they are worn down, and therefore belonged to an adult. The pelvis indicates that the individual was female and the leg bones suggest that she walked upright. It is thought that the hobbit is not a *Homo sapiens* (a modern day human) as it has very long arms and a small head the size of a grapefruit. Some of her head features represent those of a human species called *Homo erectus*, thought to have lived on a nearby island around 1.5 million years ago. However, her tiny size, similar to that of a three-year old child, suggests that she is our first glimpse of a new species of human being.

Scientists have named the new species *Homo floresiensis*. Amazingly, *Homo floresiensis* is thought to have lived as recently as 18,000 years ago, which in evolutionary terms is practically yesterday. Since the original find, bones and teeth from six other individuals have been discovered.

▶ **This is the cave in which the 'hobbit' was found on the island of Flores.**

SIZE AND TOOLS

Homo floresiensis' tiny size may be a result of being confined on an isolated island with few food resources. In addition, size and strength are less important on an island where there are few large predators. On Flores, the only large predator was the Komodo dragon.

▼ ***Homo floresiensis'* skull (top) compared with a modern-day human's skull (bottom).**

Scientists hope to unravel the mystery of *Homo floresiensis* and in particular uncover the origins of the most baffling characteristic – its small brain size. Sophisticated tools have been unearthed which seem far beyond the scope of *Homo floresiensis'* tiny brain. Scientists are still studying the bones and hope to extract DNA to help solve the puzzle and place *Homo floresiensis* in evolutionary history.

▼ An artist's impression of *Homo floresiensis*.

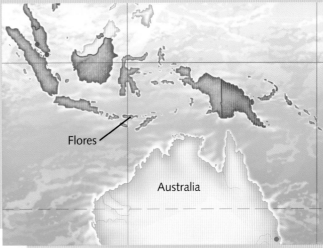

▲ The island of Flores is in Indonesia.

CONTROVERSY

There are those who doubt whether the bones represent a new human species. Certain medical conditions cause stunted growth in *Homo sapiens*, and some scientists have suggested that this accounts for the tiny body size and adult teeth. Other researchers think that it could be a diseased form of *Homo erectus*, or an individual that was deprived of food. However, since more than one specimen has been discovered, these theories seem unlikely. Quite where this species came from, and how it got to Flores remains a mystery and will be a topic of research for many years to come.

LEGENDARY TALES?

Today's inhabitants of the island of Flores tell folk stories of little people called Ebu Gogo, which translates as 'the grandmother who eats anything'. They describe Ebu Gogo as being one metre tall, hairy and prone to communicate either through murmuring or through repeating parrot-fashion what others have said to them. Some scientists speculate as to whether these legends are based on truth and have even suggested that the little species is still in existence. Whether or not *Homo floresiensis* is proved to be a unique species that co-exists with us today, evolutionists are slowly unravelling the story of human evolution.

9

Extinction

When a whole species dies out, we say that it has become extinct. Extinction is usually a natural process and it is estimated that 99.9 per cent of all species that have ever lived are now extinct. For many species, the process of extinction takes so long that new species evolve before the original species disappears. However, extinction can also occur as a direct result of man's actions and today there are many precious creatures on the brink of being wiped out.

NATURAL EXTINCTION

In nature, species become extinct when they reach the end of their evolutionary period on Earth. The length of this period depends on how well a species adjusts to changes in climate, habitat, predators and food sources. Natural events, such as volcanic eruptions, tsunamis and sudden climate change, can cause mass extinctions if the event is on a large enough scale.

There have been several mass extinctions in Earth's history. Around 440 million years ago, over 75 per cent of all species became extinct. Primitive sea creatures were the worst affected. The cause of this extinction is thought to be a dramatic change in climate, an **ice age**, during which the Earth and everything on it froze for thousands of years. The last mass extinction occurred 65 million years ago, but smaller waves of extinctions have happened more recently. Just 11,000 years ago, two important events took place. The ice sheets from the last ice age retreated and prehistoric man entered North America from Siberia. We know that at this time, over two-thirds of North America's mammals disappeared, including the short-faced bear and the sabre-toothed cat.

MAN-MADE EXTINCTION

Today, one of the biggest threats to wildlife is man. Throughout history, humans have hunted animals for food and clothing, souvenirs and trophies. Birds with beautiful displays of brightly coloured feathers, such as parrots and birds of paradise, were killed to make attractive headdresses. Unfortunately, the birds were often killed more quickly than they could be replaced, which caused the permanent loss of many species.

▲ Some birds are hunted for their colourful feathers.

Man has also hunted animals for more obscure features, such as elephant ivory, snake skin, gorilla paws and rhinoceros horn. Each of these items is meant to bring the buyer good luck or provide them with a unique ornament to display. Some people also like to have shoes or handbags made from rare reptile skins. Importing all of these items is illegal in many countries. Man has also destroyed the habitats of many species. Large areas of the Brazilian rainforests have been cleared for farming and to obtain timber for building. This has led to the loss of untold numbers of plant and animal species. It is thought that half of the world's tropical rainforests have been cut down since 1985. The tragedy of such destruction is that these rainforests contain more than half of the world's endangered species.

▲ The number of African elephants fell from 1.2 million in the 1970s, to around 500,000 today, mainly as a result of the ivory trade.

ENDANGERED SPECIES

Some species, while not yet extinct, are in serious danger of becoming so. When activities such as hunting and habitat destruction reach a critical level, species numbers become so low that they are in danger of being made extinct – they are endangered. Currently in West and Central Africa, forest animals have been hunted for food to such an extent that many are now threatened with extinction. Approximately one million tonnes of forest animals are hunted and killed in these regions every year. One threatened species is the bonobo, which is believed to be man's closest relative.

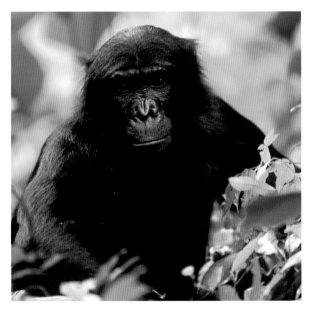

▲ Bonobos are the rarest of all the great ape species.

DID YOU KNOW?

▶ The tragic tsunami in South East Asia in December 2004 not only killed and displaced tens of thousands of people, it may also lead to extinctions. Many habitats, including mangroves, coral reefs, wetlands and forests were damaged, and fresh water lakes were poisoned by salt water.

TIME TRAVEL: DINOSAUR EXTINCTION

Dinosaurs dominated Earth for 165 million years. They ranged in size from huge, 15 metre tall creatures, to small chicken-sized animals. Around 65 million years ago there was a catastrophic event, which killed off approximately 75 per cent of life on our planet; most famously, the dinosaurs were wiped out.

HOW DID THE DINOSAURS BECOME EXTINCT?

The most widely accepted theory for dinosaur extinction is that an asteroid slammed into Earth. Evidence supporting this theory comes from studies of iridium levels in rocks. Iridium is a precious metal found in small amounts in Earth's rocks but in much higher concentrations in asteroids. Scientists have found a very thin layer of iridium in rocks worldwide, with a chemical makeup similar to that of an asteroid. An asteroid–Earth collision could have caused iridium to disperse across the globe and settle, forming this thin layer.

THE ASTEROID THEORY EXPLAINED:

(1) An asteroid from outer space crashed into the Earth. This impact may have been in the Yucatan region of Mexico where there is a crater approximately 200 kilometres wide – large enough to have caused a global catastrophe. The explosion this caused would have been 10,000 times greater than all of Earth's nuclear weapons going off at once.
(2) The impact caused massive earthquakes and tsunamis, resulting in widespread destruction at ground level.

Crater site

▲ The impact crater is half on land and half in the sea in the Yucatan region of Mexico.

(3) Hot debris was sent flying in all directions leading to forest fires and the loss of many species and their habitats.
(4) Millions of tonnes of dust and debris were thrown into the atmosphere, which began to settle over a very large area.
(5) Acidic gases were released from the damaged crust of the Earth. These entered the atmosphere, circulated the world and eventually fell as acid rain, seriously polluting water courses.
(6) Dust and debris that did not settle blocked light and heat from the Sun. The Earth's climate quickly cooled and a perishing winter set in lasting many months. Large numbers of species could not

◄ An asteroid is thought to have wiped out the dinosaurs.

survive such a sudden change in climate.
(7) Following the 'winter', a build up of carbon dioxide in the atmosphere prevented any heat left on Earth from leaving. This greenhouse effect had devastating effects on global weather patterns resulting in the extinction of yet more species.

THE CONSEQUENCES

All dinosaurs, whether they lived on land, in the sea or in the air, were made extinct. The lack of sunlight would have caused the death of most plant species. Herbivorous (plant-eating) dinosaurs would have starved and died. Carnivorous (meat-eating) dinosaurs fed on herbivorous dinosaurs, and would have also starved. Dinosaurs needed sunlight to keep warm – a further factor making their survival impossible. The survivors were mostly small mammals, birds and fish that were able to adapt to the new conditions on Earth. As with all mass extinctions, there was a sudden evolutionary burst of new species to fill Earth's new habitats.

MEGA VOLCANOES

Not everyone accepts the asteroid theory. Around 65 million years ago, there was extreme volcanic activity across the world. Volcanoes spewed dust and acidic chemicals into the atmosphere and this may have changed the Earth's climate enough to trigger a mass extinction. The only way we are likely to ever know for certain is if we could travel back in time.

COULD IT HAPPEN AGAIN?

Mass extinction events have occurred regularly throughout Earth's history. Researchers estimate that they occur every 26 to 30 million years, possibly as a result of collisions with a cloud of comets, called the Oort cloud, crossing Earth's path. Whilst a mass extinction event is highly likely, we are pretty safe for the time being, or at least the next 10 million years.

▼ Could volcanic activity have killed the dinosaurs?

10

Classification

As a result of evolution there are millions of species living on Earth today. Our planet supports all of these species, and scientists are finding new ones all the time. It is easy to tell the difference between some species, such as between an oak tree and a wheat plant, whereas others look very similar, such as African and Indian elephants. A system of classification allows biologists to name all species.

FIVE KINGDOMS

There are five main kingdoms: animals, plants, prokaryotes, protists and fungi. Each kingdom is split into several phyla. Each phylum group contains organisms that have features in common.

THE ANIMAL KINGDOM

The animal kingdom is divided into invertebrates (organisms without a backbone) and vertebrates (organisms with a backbone).

▲▼ This crab (above) and this beetle (below) are invertebrates. They have no backbone.

INVERTEBRATES

PHYLUM	FEATURES
Cnidarians	Sac-like body with tentacles (for example, a jellyfish)
Flatworms	Flat body with a mouth at one end
Roundworms	Long thread-like body
Segmented worms	Body divided into segments (for example, an earthworm)
Molluscs	Carry a shell and have a muscular 'foot' (for example, a snail)
Echinoderms	Contain five parts and have spiny skins (for example, a sea urchin)
Arthropods – crustaceans	Chalk-like exoskeleton (for example, a crab)
Arthropods – myriapods	Segmented bodies and many pairs of legs (for example, a millipede)
Arthropods – insects	Body in three parts, three pairs of legs and two pairs of wings (for example, a beetle)
Arthropods – arachnids	Body in two parts, four pairs of legs (for example, a spider)

VERTEBRATES

This puffin is in the animal kingdom, is a vertebrate and belongs to the bird phylum.

PHYLUM	FEATURES
Birds	Have feathers, wings and lungs, lay eggs
Fish	Live in water, have scaly skin, fins and gills
Amphibians	Moist skin and live on land and in water, lay eggs in water (for example, a frog)
Reptiles	Dry, scaly skin, breed on land, lay eggs with shells (for example, a lizard)
Mammals	Have hair or fur, have lungs, young grow inside the mother who has mammary glands on which young can suckle

THE PLANT KINGDOM

▼ Moss

PHYLUM	FEATURES
Ferns	Have strong stems and roots and spores on the underside of the leaves
Conifers	Keep their needle-like leaves throughout the winter
Flowering plants	Produce flowers that contain the reproductive organs and produce seeds
Mosses and liverworts	Live in damp places and do not have a proper stem or roots

THE PROKARYOTES, PROTISTS AND FUNGI KINGDOMS

KINGDOM	FEATURES
Prokaryotes	No proper nucleus and can only be seen with a microscope (for example, bacteria)
Protists	Have a proper nucleus, can be single or multi-celled, live in water (for example, algae) or inside other organisms
Fungi	Made up of thin threads called hyphae, produce spores (for example, a mushroom)

▲ These mushrooms are in the fungi kingdom.

TEST YOURSELF

▶ For each of the following organisms, decide to which kingdom and where possible, to which phylum, they belong:
Apple trees

Crocodiles
Eagles
Sea urchins
Bread mould

CLASSIFYING ORGANISMS

Phyla are divided into smaller groups, which themselves have subcategories. This system is used by biologists to classify any living organism. Each of the smaller divisions is shown in the table below for two species of rat. Both are common rats; however the black rat is famous for transmitting the 'bubonic plague', which killed millions of people in Europe during the 1300s. The brown rat carries other diseases such as salmonella.

The black and the brown rat belong to the same kingdom, phylum, class, order, family and genus. They share many features. They each have mammalian characteristics such as fur and mammary glands. Both species have rodent characteristics such as a gestation period of roughly 22 days and the ability to produce between four and seven litters in one year.

▲ Brown rats

However, there are subtle differences between these two rats, which means that they are different species and cannot breed together to give fertile offspring. The black rat has slate black fur whereas that of the brown rat is red-brown. The black rat has pointed ears and a long nose, whereas the ears of the brown rat are more rounded and the nose is a little shorter.

▼ Black rat

	BLACK RAT	**BROWN RAT**
KINGDOM	Animal	Animal
PHYLUM	Vertebrate	Vertebrate
CLASS	Mammalia	Mammalia
ORDER	Rodentia	Rodentia
FAMILY	Muridae	Muridae
GENUS	*Rattus*	*Rattus*
SPECIES	*rattus*	*norvegicus*

DID YOU KNOW?

▶ The system of naming was introduced by a Swedish biologist called Carolus Linnaeus in his book called 'Systemae Naturae' in which he gave all living organisms a two-part name that was based on their features. Human beings are named *Homo sapiens*.

TAXONOMY AND KEYS

Biologists who study classification are called **taxonomists** and they identify species by asking questions. For example, if you wanted to identify whether an organism is a prokaryote, you could ask the following question:

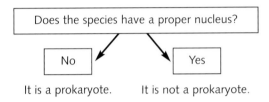

This diagram is called a key and is only composed of one simple question. However, keys can be extended to include a whole series of questions, all with 'yes' or 'no' answers. Imagine we had five animals that needed to be identified – a snail, mouse, frog, jellyfish and earthworm. The following key could be used:

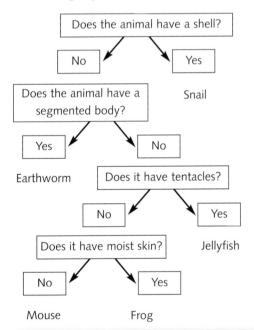

The questions do not need to be set out as a diagram. They can be listed, as shown below:

(1)   Does the animal have a shell?
        Yes .... it is a snail
        No .... go to Q2

(2)   Does the animal have a segmented body?
        Yes .... it is an earthworm
        No .... go to Q3

(3)   Does the animal have tentacles?
        Yes .... it is a jellyfish
        No .... go to Q4

(4)   Does the animal have moist skin?
        Yes .... it is a frog
        No .... it is a mouse

We do not have to memorise every detail about an organism in order to identify it. Instead we use a key as a short cut. The system of classification is continually being modified as new information and species are discovered. Organisms are moved from one genus to another as scientists make new observations. This improves our knowledge of the classification system and the living world.

▲ Keys are used to identify organisms.

TEST YOURSELF

▶ Choose five objects in your school bag and write a key to allow someone it identify them. Try your key out on your friends.

▶ Choose five of your friends and write a key to identify them.

Glossary

ALLELE – A variant of a gene. An allele is a member of a pair or series of genes that code for a particular feature, such as eye colour or hair colour.

ARTIFICIAL SELECTION – When humans deliberately reproduce plants or animals so that desirable traits are represented in later generations.

CELLS – The tiny building blocks that make up living organisms. Each cell contains a nucleus, which is the control centre of the cell.

CHROMOSOME – A thread of DNA found in a cell's nucleus.

CLONING – The creation of an individual who is genetically identical to the parent. Identical twins are clones, but clones can also be produced by genetic engineering.

CONTINUOUS VARIATION – Variation in characteristics that can not be put into one category or another, but instead range from one extreme to the other. The changes are slight and overlap so much that they are thought of as being continuous, such as height or weight.

DISCONTINUOUS VARIATION – Variation in a characteristic that can be placed in one category or another, such as blood group.

EMBRYOLOGY – Study of the formation and development of organisms from a zygote, or fertilised egg.

EVOLUTION – The process by which all living things change slowly over millions of years. The change occurs because of slight variations in the genetic make up that one generation passes on to the next.

EXTINCT – This is when a species or group of species ceases to exist.

FOSSILS – The remains of living things, or their imprints, that have been left in rocks over a very long period of time.

GENE POOL – All the genes in a population of organisms at any one time.

GENES – Specific segments of DNA on a chromosome that describe an individual's features.

ANSWERS

P7 Investigate
Your graph should have shoe size on the horizontal axis and the number of people on the vertical axis. If five people had size seven shoes, for example, you would draw a horizontal line from '5' and a vertical line from '7'. Where the two lines meet you draw a cross. When you have done this for all of the different shoe sizes, draw a line and connect all of the crosses. This should give you a normal distribution curve, which is a bell shaped curve (right).

P7 Test yourself
Weight and IQ are examples of continuous variation.
Gender, attached and free earlobes, eye colour, and the ability or inability to hyper-extend the thumb (hitch hiker's thumb) are all examples of discontinuous variation.

P17 Investigate
The 'tall' allele (T) is dominant to the 'dwarf' (t) allele.
If you cross Tt and Tt, 75 per cent of the offspring are tall plants and 25 per cent are dwarf plants.
If you cross TT and tt, 100 per cent of the offspring are tall.
If you cross TT and Tt, 100 per cent of the offspring are tall.

P23 Investigate
To ensure the long-term continuation of their species:
(1) Lions have grown bigger and stronger and are able to run fast. Their pale fur is good camouflage against the grassy plains on which

GENOTYPE – The genetic make up of an organism.

ICE AGE – A time period that lasts thousands of years during which the Earth is very cold. During an ice age, massive ice sheets cover much of Earth's Northern Hemisphere.

MUTATION – A change in the amount or arrangement of genetic material in a cell.

NATURAL SELECTION – The process in nature by which only the organisms best adapted to their environment survive and pass their genetic information on to the next generation.

NORMAL DISTRIBUTION CURVE – This is a bell-shaped curve on a graph formed by plotting information that is normally distributed. This means that fewer individuals have extreme characteristics, such as a very large or very small foot size. Most individuals have characteristics that fall between the two extremes, such as medium-sized feet.

PHENOTYPE – The physical appearance of an individual that is determined by the genes and the environment.

PSEUDOGENES – Naturally occurring genes that are altered in some way so that they do not have a function.

SPECIATION – The formation of a new species through evolution.

SPECIES – A group of organisms that can breed freely with one other, but not with members of other species. For example, cows are one species and pigs are another.

STEM CELLS – Unspecialised, immature cells that are capable of developing into any type of cell in the body. Stem cells are found in embryos and are called embryonic stem cells. Adult stem cells are also found in some parts of the adult body.

TAXONOMISTS – Scientists who deal with the identification, naming and classification of living things.

Useful websites:

www.bbc.co.uk/schools
www.nationalgeographic.com
www.sciencenewsforkids.org
www.newscientist.com
www.howstuffworks.com

they live. This allows them to remain undetected while they stalk and catch prey.

(2) Chameleons have developed the ability to change colour. They do this to communicate with each other, for example when they want to mate. Because this communication encourages mating it could be viewed as a factor that helps the species to survive.

P29 Test yourself
Animal kingdom: Chickens can be selected for their ability to lay large eggs. This is done to increase profits made through the sale of eggs. How is it done? Chickens that lay the biggest eggs are crossed. The female offspring that produce the largest eggs are selected and bred again. The process is repeated until a large proportion of a generation produce large eggs.

Plant kingdom: Fruit trees are selected for dwarf varieties that can be grown in pots. This makes them easy to transport and allows those them to be grown in small gardens.

P43 Test yourself
Apple trees = Plant kingdom, flowering plants
Crocodiles = Animal kingdom, reptiles
Eagle = Animal kingdom, birds
Sea urchin = Animal kingdom, echinoderms
Bread mould = Fungi kingdom

P45 Test yourself
Example key for a pen, pencil, book, calculator and a door key.
(1) Can you write with it? YES – Go to Q2. NO – Go to Q3.
(2) Is the writing grey? YES – It is a pencil. NO – It is a pen.
(3) Does it have pages in it? YES – It is a book. NO – Go to Q4.
(4) Does it have buttons? YES – It is a calculator. NO – It is a door key.

Index

Page references in italics represent pictures.

Photo Credits – (abbv: r, right, l, left, t, top, m, middle, b, bottom) **Front cover images** Fotolia **p.1** (tr) www.istockphoto.com/Daniel Goodchild (bl) www.istockphoto.com/Ingvald Kaldhussæter (br) www.istockphoto.com/Jeroen Peys **p.2** www.istockphoto.com/Ewa Brozek **p.3** (t) www.istockphoto.com/blaneyphoto (b) www.istockphoto.com/Ana Abejon **p.4** (tl) www.istockphoto.com/Jason van der Valk (tr) www.istockphoto.com/Bob Ainsworth (br) www.istockphoto.com/Steve McWilliam **p.5** www.istockphoto.com/lamprey **p.6** Jose Luis Pelaez, Inc./Corbis **p.8** (t) Yann Arthus-Bertrand/Corbis (m) www.istockphoto.com/Fanelie Rosier (b) www.istockphoto.com/Stephanie Asher **p.9** (t) www.istockphoto.com/lamprey (b) www.istockphoto.com/Charleen Cole **p.10** (t) www.istockphoto.com/Ana Abejon (b) Andrew Harrington/naturepl.com **p.11** (t) www.istockphoto.com/Judi Ashlock (b) Philippe Clement/naturepl.com **p.12** Weill Rachel/Oxford Scientific **p.13** Ian Boddy/Science Photo Library **p.14** James King-Holmes/Science Photo Library **p.15** www.istockphoto.com/Ewa Brozek **p.16** (l) www.istockphoto.com/John Kerher (r) www.istockphoto.com/Louis Aguinaldo **p.17** Kit Houghton/Corbis **p.18** Science Photo Library **p.20** (t) US Department of Energy Genome Programs http://doegenomes.org (b) Louie Psihoyos/Corbis **p.21** Dr G Moscoso/Science Photo Library **p.22** David Fox/Oxford Scientific **p.23** Ifa-Bilderteam Gmbh/Oxford Scientific (b) Gulin Darrell/Oxford Scientific **p.24** Doug Allan/Oxford Scientific **p.25** (t) Science Photo Library (b) Mary Plage/Oxford Scientific **p.26** www.istockphoto.com/Ingvald Kaldhussæter **p.27** (t) www.istockphoto.com/Daniel Goodchild (b) Robert Dowling/Corbis **p.28** www.istockphoto.com/Stephanie Phillips **p.29** Irene Plyusnina/Current Biology **p.31** (t) www.istockphoto.com/Andrei Tchernov (b) Klaus Guldbrandsen/Science Photo Library **p.32** (t) www.istockphoto.com/Bob Ainsworth (b) Kevin Schafer/Corbis **p.33** (t) Mike Powles/Oxford Scientific (b) www.istockphoto.com/Jeroen Peys **p.34** (l) Daniel Sambraus/Science Photo Library (m) Steve Allen/Science Photo Library (r) Oxford Scientific **p.35** (t) www.istockphoto.com/Maciej Sekowski (b) Dan Shapiro/NOAA **p.36** (l) Reuters/Corbis (r) Rex Features **p.37** reproduced with the permission of Peter Schouten/National Geographic Society **p.38** www.istockphoto.com/Lisa F Young **p.39** (t) Reuters/Corbis (b) Martyn Colbeck/Oxford Scientific **p.40** (tr) NASA (tl) Courtesy NASA/JPL-Caltech **p.41** Zephyr/Science Photo Library **p.42** (t) www.istockphoto.com/Jason van der Valk (b) www.istockphoto.com/Eric Gagnon **p.43** (t) David Tipling/Oxford Scientific (m) www.istockphoto.com/David Freund (b) www.istockphoto.com/blaneyphoto **p.44** (t) Robin Redfern/Oxford Scientific (b) Bert & Babs Wells/Oxford Scientific **p.45** www.istockphoto.com/Steve McWilliam